W9-BTB-014

DATE DUE

Veterinarians Help Us

Aaron R. Murray

Enslow Elementary

an imprint of

Enslow Publishers, Inc.

40 Industrial Road
Box 398
Berkeley Heights, NJ 07922
USA

http://www.enslow.com

Enslow Elementary, an imprint of Enslow Publishers, Inc.
Enslow Elementary® is a registered trademark of Enslow Publishers, Inc.

Library of Congress Cataloging-in-Publication Data
Murray, Aaron R.
  Veterinarians help us / Aaron R. Murray.
     p. cm. — (All about community helpers)
  Summary: "Introduces pre-readers to simple concepts about what veterinarians do using short
sentences and repetition of words"— Provided by publisher.
  Includes bibliographical references and index.
  ISBN 978-0-7660-4046-5
  1. Veterinarians—Juvenile literature. 2. Veterinary medicine—Juvenile literature. I. Title.
  SF756.M87 2012
  636.089—dc23
                              2011031049
Future editions:
Paperback ISBN 978-1-4644-0054-4
ePUB ISBN 978-1-4645-0961-2
PDF ISBN 978-1-4646-0961-9

Printed in the United States of America
032012 Lake Book Manufacturing, Inc., Melrose Park, IL
10 9 8 7 6 5 4 3 2 1

To Our Readers: We have done our best to make sure all Internet Addresses in this book were active
and appropriate when we went to press. However, the author and the publisher have no control over and
assume no liability for the material available on those Internet sites or on other Web sites they may link
to. Any comments or suggestions can be sent by e-mail to comments@enslow.com or to the address on
the back cover.

♲ Enslow Publishers, Inc., is committed to printing our books on recycled paper. The paper in every
book contains 10% to 30% post-consumer waste (PCW). The cover board on the outside of each book
contains 100% PCW. Our goal is to do our part to help young people and the environment too!

Photo Credits: All photos Shutterstock.com except © iStockphoto.com: kali9, pp. 4, 20; Valerie
Loiseleux, p. 8; DenGuy, p. 10; Mark Hatfield, p. 16; Thye Aun Ngo, p 18; Carmen Martínez Banús,
p. 22.
Cover Photo: kali9/iStockphoto.com

Note to Parents and Teachers
Help pre-readers get a jump-start on reading. These lively stories introduce simple concepts with
repetition of words and short, simple sentences. Photos and illustrations fill the pages with color and
effectively enhance the text. Free Educator Guides are available for this series at www.enslow.com.
Search for the *All About Community Helpers* series name.

Contents

Words to Know

farm   **medicine**   **sick**

A veterinarian is a doctor for animals.

A veterinarian is also called a vet.

Vets go to school to learn how to take care of animals.

Vets help all kinds of animals.

**Vets know
about medicine.**

Some vets help zoo animals.

Some vets help farm animals.

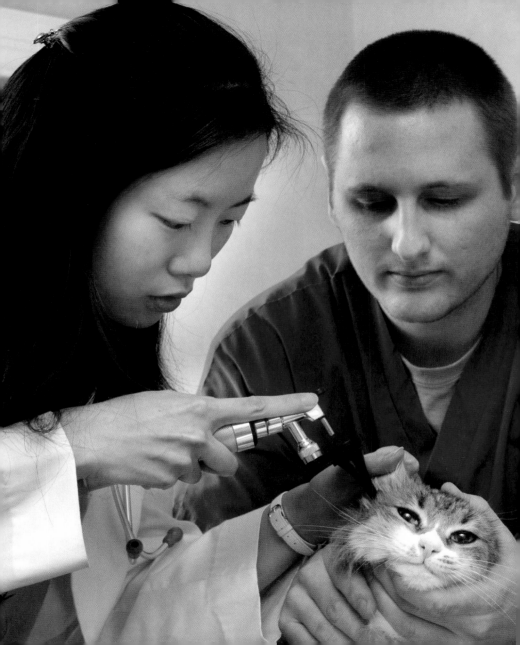

Some vets help pets
when they are hurt.

Some vets help pets
when they are sick.

Vets help animals get better.

Vets help find good homes for pets.

Do you like helping animals?

You may want to be a vet.

Read More

Ames, Michelle. *Veterinarians in Our Community*. New York: PowerKids Press, 2009.

Leake, Diyan. *Vets*. Chicago: Heinemann Raintree, 2008.

Macken, JoAnn Early. *Veterinarians*. New York: Gareth Stevens Publishing, 2010.

Web Sites

FutureVet: Kids
<http://futurevet.net/kids/welcome/>

Care for Animals: Petpourri
<http://www.avma.org/careforanimals/kidscorner/default.asp>

Index

Guided Reading Level: C
Guided Reading Leveling System is based on the guidelines recommended by Fountas and Pinnell.

Word Count: 86